EDITING MANGA

EDITING MANGA

Working with Translations in a Visual Medium

By Jan Mitsuko Cash

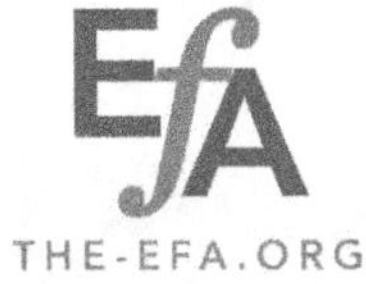

266 West 37th St., 20th Floor
New York, NY 10018
info@the-efa.org

ISBN paperback   978-1-880407-54-7
ISBN ebook   978-1-880407-55-4

Cash, Jan Mitsuko. *Editing Manga: Working with Translations in a Visual Medium*
An EFA Booklet: Published in the United States of America by the Editorial Freelancers Association.

Subject Categories: Editing & Proofreading | Communication Studies | Business Skills | Art Techniques

Legal Disclaimer

While the publisher and author have made every attempt to verify that the information provided in this book is correct and up to date, the publisher and author assume no responsibility for any error, inaccuracy, or omission.

The advice, examples, and strategies contained herein are not suitable for every situation. Neither the publisher nor author shall be liable for damages arising therefrom. This book is not intended for use as a source of legal or financial advice. Running a business involves complex legal and financial issues. You should always retain competent legal and financial professionals to provide guidance.

EFA Publications Chairperson: Robin Martin
Copyeditor: Heidi Ward
Proofreader: Ronane Lloyd
Book Designer: Stephanie Argy
Cover Designer: Robot House

See more by the author:
Jan Mitsuko Cash
janmitsuko.cash
twitter.com/Jmitsu
linkedin.com/in/jancash

Contents

Dedication

◇◇◇◇◇

To Vincent and my mother, who have both been much too reasonable considering my unreasonable career.

Introduction

The manga market has rapidly grown with the popularity of anime and other Japanese media, even at times when overall book sales have been down, yet few training materials currently exist for those hoping to enter the industry. This booklet will teach new as well as experienced editors the fundamentals of manga editing and how to work with translated text in the context of a visual medium. While this booklet will focus on Japanese comics, much of the information contained in it will also be applicable to manhwa (Korean comics), manhua (Chinese comics), and English-language comics.

As manga editing is specialized and relatively new in the context of publishing, many editors learn on the job, and every publisher's list of qualifications differ. Conversely, because no singular route into the manga industry exists, simply becoming familiar with the current publishing standards and common issues that occur when reworking Japanese comics for a new audience in a different language can give one a leg up.

What This Booklet Will Cover

This booklet will cover some steps within manga workflows to give you context to make informed choices when working with translators and letterers. It will also go over some common manga standards that often go unnoticed by those who have not worked in the industry.

It will also cover manga-specific concepts and terminology, style guidelines that differ from prose and Chicago style, and visual aspects of manga that need to be taken into account along with the textual elements.

By the end of this booklet, you'll have an understanding of the basics of manga creation, and you'll know what elements of manga to keep an eye on when taking tests or editing manga for a publisher. It'll conclude with some advice about seeking manga jobs and further resources for self-study.

What Is Manga?

Manga are simply comics that originate from Japan. They are not limited by genre, target audience, or art style, though most manga are printed in black and white.

While Western comics tend to be created by a team of people who each fulfill separate roles to write, draw, letter, and color a single comic, manga are usually credited to a single creator or a writer-artist duo who may employ a small team of uncredited assistant artists for help. Manga turnarounds are often very quick, but they are serialized a chapter at a time, similar to Western comics.

The publication process also differs from Western releases: instead of publishing each chapter as a standalone booklet, single chapters of multiple manga series are bundled together into magazines targeted toward a demographic. Production is weekly or monthly for many of the larger magazines, and most manga are printed solely in black and white or with a limited number of color pages. Once enough chapters of a series have been published through serialization, they are collected and published as a print volume called a *tankobon* (often called *tanko* or *tanks* by English publishers).

When translated, most manga are published a volume at a time, but English publishers have recently begun to publish *simulpubs* (simultaneous publications) by digitally distributing single chapters on publisher websites or on subscription-based manga apps at the same time they are released in Japan. The English publisher will often later collect these simulpubbed chapters into a volume format to be distributed digitally or in print, similar to the tankobon in Japan.

These simulpubs are often fast-paced, only allotting from a few days to a week per chapter, so in-house editors do most of the editorial work. However, some publishers have begun to publish manga a chapter at a time, independent of the publishing schedule in Japan. Publishers that focus on these nonsimultaneous chapter releases and per-volume releases have fewer schedule restraints and are more likely to hire freelance editors.

The Manga Workflow: Steps by Role

◇◇◇◇◇

Manga publisher workflows vary, so the number and order of steps a manga goes through from licensing to publication will depend on which publisher you are working with. Many steps in the localization pipeline are associated directly with work done by an individual, thus we'll go over some common roles involved in manga. In practice, these steps can be done in different orders and some editing steps might be fulfilled exclusively by in-house employees or skipped entirely.

Licensing

The English-language publisher will make an offer to the Japanese publisher of a manga and pay a licensing fee to obtain the rights to publish a translated version of the work. The *licensor* is the Japanese publisher and the *licensee* is the English publisher creating the translation. In-house employees handle licensing, though freelancers can sometimes make licensing suggestions. This process has no defined timeline, as decisions are dependent upon the Japanese publisher.

Translation

The publisher hires a freelancer to translate the manga from Japanese to English. The translator will typically deliver a text-based script to the publisher.

Adaptation

An editor "punches up" the script to make it entertaining to read. This is sometimes also handled by the translator or is part of the in-house editor's duties. Some publishers hire freelance rewriters.

Lettering

Text from the script is laid out on top of the art along with sound effects and background-text translations. This is typically done by a freelance *letterer* (sometimes called a *typesetter* by manhwa and manhua publishers).

Copyediting

An editor checks the manga for grammar, spelling, and other technical issues. Sometimes this role is combined with adaptation. Some publishers have copyeditors work with a text-based script, while others work with the manga after lettering has been completed. This role can be in-house or freelance depending on the publisher.

Proofreading

An editor checks the lettered version of the book after it has been edited in order to catch any remaining errors that need to be corrected prior to publication. Some publishers will provide an EPUB file and will ask for a text file listing all corrections, while others will provide a PDF for markup or ask that the proofing be done in a third-party tool. This role is often freelance, though it can also be done by in-house editors.

Some publishers will skip certain roles, such as adaptation. Though editing at the script stage is common at many manga publishers, the translated script may be lettered prior to editing so the text is alongside the artwork as a reader would see it.

In addition, while in-house editors usually communicate directly with freelancers, freelance editors are not always connected with other freelancers on the same project. Some publishers will be happy to introduce a freelance team to each other when asked, but others prefer an in-house employee to act as a go-between. If you are working as a freelancer, it's important to note that you might not receive direct answers to your queries or be the one resolving issues within a script after submitting your work.

> Some publishers will call proofreading or translation checks QA (quality assurance) or QC (quality check). You might also come across the term LQA, which is "linguistic/language quality assurance" and often refers to a translation check. Some newer manga publishers will also use the term proofreader when they mean a copyeditor or rewriter, so it's important to check in about your expected duties when applying or once hired.

The Anatomy of a Manga

◇◇◇◇◇

Scripts break manga down into their component parts, so you'll need to know some print and comics terminology to understand how to read a text script and work with lettered pages.

Page Layout

First, when a book is opened, the two facing pages are called a *spread*. The boxed elements within a comic are called *panels*, and the text within these consists of bubbles (also called balloons), sound effects, captions, asides, and other pieces of text. The space between panels is called the *gutter*.

> Most manga are meant to be read in spread format. In some cases, text or panels span the entire spread, so editing a manga one page at a time can result in major errors or the narrative being read out of order.

Japanese books are read right to left, and translated manga generally keep this reading order. Each panel and element within the page is also read right to left, as is Japanese text that is written vertically, though horizontal text is read left to right.

What Are Balloons or Bubbles?

The two most common types of text containers are captions and balloons (or *bubbles*). Captions are typically used for narration or internal thoughts, while bubbles are used for both character dialogue and thoughts. Another common type of element is a *burst*.

Tails, the pointy nubs on bubbles, are used to indicate the speaker of dialogue. Western comics require a balloon tail, but manga are more flexible in this regard. Most manga tails are very short or

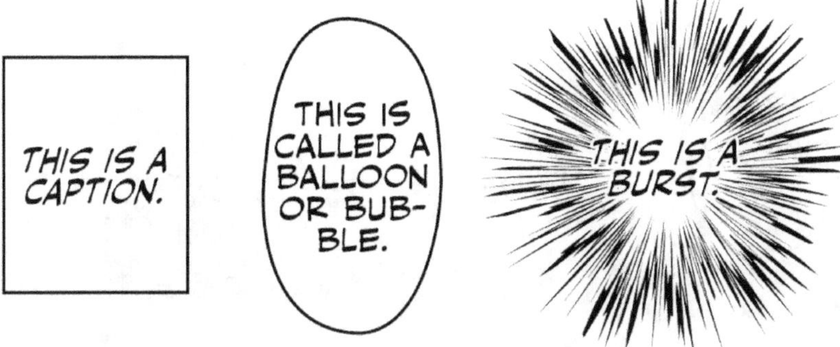

Figure 1: A caption is enclosed within a box while balloons or bubbles are round shapes. Bursts are shaped like lines emanating from one central point.

nonexistent. When a character is on the opposite side of the panel from their dialogue or another character intervenes between them and the dialogue, bubbles will sometimes drop the tail entirely. An inward-facing tail can be used to indicate

The Western comics industry only uses the term balloons and will flinch at every use of bubble in much the same way some style guides insist alright is not a word. The manga industry is looser with terminology and most letterers and publishers will use the term bubble or even alright.

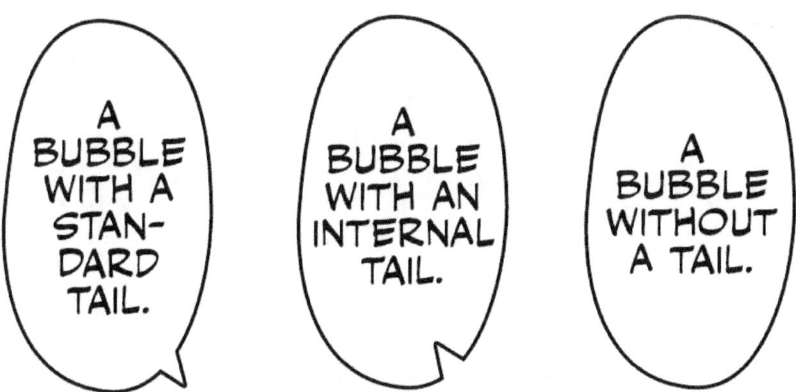

Figure 2: Three styles of bubbles with and without tails.

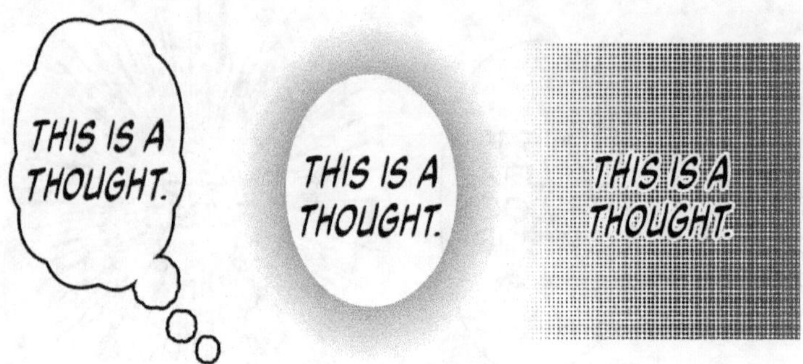

Figure 3: Three examples of thoughts or internal narration. The rightmost example uses a white stroke to make the letters stand out against the screentone.

an off-screen character is speaking. These are common in manhua and manhwa as well.

Likewise, internal character monologues have fewer restrictions compared with Western comics. While thought balloons are used in manga, thoughts and internal narration can also be free floating within a panel and have no container at all. Instead, they are typeset right over the screentone (texture and patterns in the background).

Most publishers will ask for thoughts to be italicized. When a thought is set against a background without a bubble, the letterer can apply a white stroke around the letters to make the text legible.

Manga Fonts

Manga usually follow Western comic conventions when translated, so dialogue fonts are in all caps and center aligned. Serif fonts are sometimes used for narration, which may be in mixed case. But they should not be used for dialogue.

When using emphasis, comics typically use bold italics rather than just italics. When a word preceding ending punctuation is emphasized, the punctuation should generally be in bold italics as well.

If you are working with a publisher without font preferences or style guidelines, a good rule of thumb is to avoid cliché font choices, such as Comic Sans, Papyrus, and the like. Wild Words is likely the most common font choice used in manga, but several other comic fonts exist. Comicraft and Blambot are good places to take a look at dialogue fonts, and some manga letterers create and distribute their

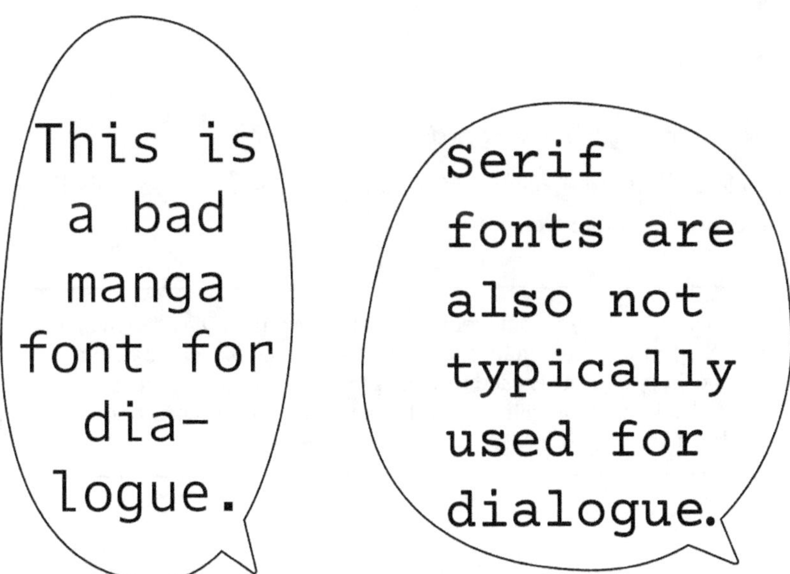

Figure 4: Mixed-case and serif fonts are not used in manga dialogue.

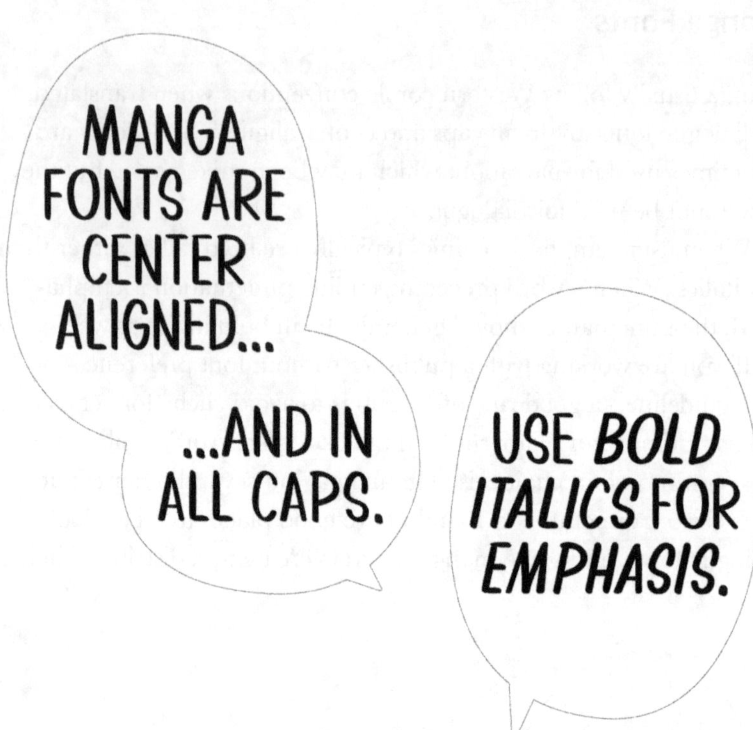

Figure 5: An example of a more typical manga font.

own fonts that are specialized for manga use as well. Appendix B has direct links to some websites.

Not all fonts are free. Some require different licensing fees depending on how the font is used. If a font that isn't part of a publisher's style guide or repository of fonts is used in a manga you are editing, it may be a good idea to check in with your in-house contact to make sure the font has been licensed for use.

Scripting Your Way to Success

$\diamond\diamond\diamond\diamond\diamond$

Though each publisher has its own script format, the general elements are typically the same from company to company:

- *Labels* – A brief descriptor of the speaker, sound effect, or some other textual element on the page. This is used for informative purposes and will not appear in the published manga.
- *Text* – The text to be typeset or lettered on the page of the manga.
- *Notes* – Additional notes that are passed from one individual to another. These often include information about the location of a sound effect or additional context the next person in a workflow will need. Notes can be included as comment balloons or within the text of the script. They are often bracketed, highlighted, or colored red. These notes are *not* the same as translation notes or endnotes, as they are for internal use only.

Most scripts are broken down by page and panel numbers, and the text elements appear according to their reading order on a page. When editing from a script, you will need to keep the Japanese version of the manga open alongside the English script to see how each element maps on the page.

The most common script format is column-based, where tabs or tables are used to separate the script labels from the text that needs to be lettered. Table-style scripts are functionally the same, though they have borders between each line and column.

Other script formats are closer to Western comic-style scripts, which are in a linear text format where each element is on a new line and labels are distinguished using bold or italics. Most letterers and

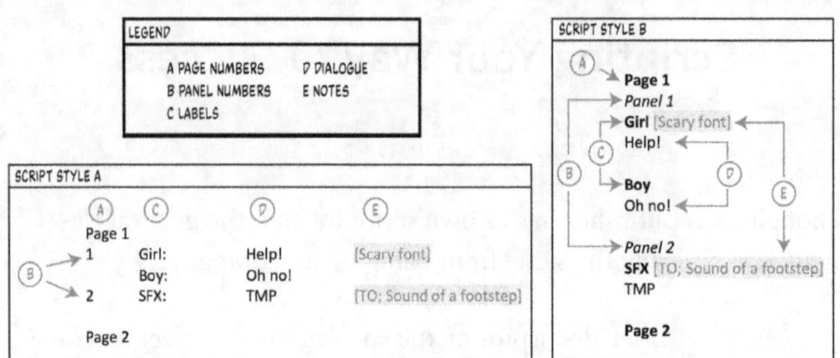

Figure 6: Two examples of scripts. Script A is a column-based script, while Script B is a Western-style script.

translators prefer a column-based script with as little formatting as possible, but the publisher ultimately determines the script style.

Manga formats are designed to make the transition from a text document to lettering within typesetting software more efficient, so deviating from a script format can create issues for others down the line. Make sure to follow column-based and table-based script for-

New editors will sometimes fall into the trap of only focusing on the text, but the true heart of manga is in the art! Keep the Japanese version of the manga open when looking at a script, and look out for missing translations, which are more common than you might expect.

mats carefully, as these are often designed so that a letterer can delete columns to isolate the dialogue from other parts of the script.

Common Comic Convention Deviations

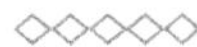

Comic books have a tradition separate from *The Chicago Manual of Style*. Most departures vary from publisher to publisher, but the same issues usually come up within every style guide. This section will cover some common situations with examples.

Numbers

Most publishers will spell out only numbers zero through ten and multiples of one hundred. There are, however, two additional considerations that need to be made with manga: one is whether a spelled-out number will fit within the bubble, and the other is how the number will look alongside all-caps letters.

In some cases, readability and bubble fit will need to be prioritized over style.

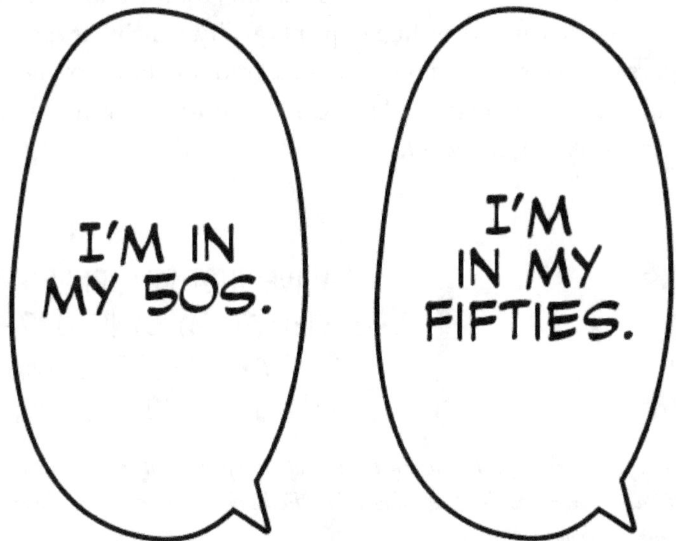

Figure 7: When written out in numeral form, 50s may look like SOS.

Midword Breaks

Breaks within words should follow standard proofreading guidelines—in other words, hyphens should land in between syllables, just as they would in prose text. If possible, the word shouldn't be broken, though this isn't always possible due to bubble sizes.

Hyphens occur more commonly in manga because of the balloon widths, which are made to fit a language that's read vertically rather than horizontally. Hyphens are a reality of manga and shouldn't (or rather, *can't*) be entirely avoided, as they are often the least distracting solution for words that won't fit within a tight space. One way to help make word breaking easier for letterers is to avoid contractions within very tight spaces, as these are difficult or impossible to break naturally.

Crossbar I Versus Slash I: Getting Personal

Western comics have historically used a *crossbar I* for all instances of the personal pronoun *I* because of print limitations. Though modern printers are capable of higher print quality, which has rendered crossbars unnecessary in most situations, tradition has kept the crossbar I alive even in manga publishing. In contrast, other instances of the letter *I* will use the *slash I*.

Figure 8: A crossbar I (left) has horizontal lines at the top and bottom of the letter, while a slash I (center) is simply a straight line. To the right is an example of both forms of the letter in action.

The slash I may also be used in cases where an I could be mistaken for another glyph, such as in vertical-set text.

Punctuation Oddities: Commas, Quotation Marks, and Ending Punctuation

Translators will sometimes attempt to mimic the exact punctuation of the original Japanese. This usually isn't desirable since ending punctuation is optional in Japanese dialogue balloons, and commas and other types of punctuation marks have entirely different grammatical functions compared to English.

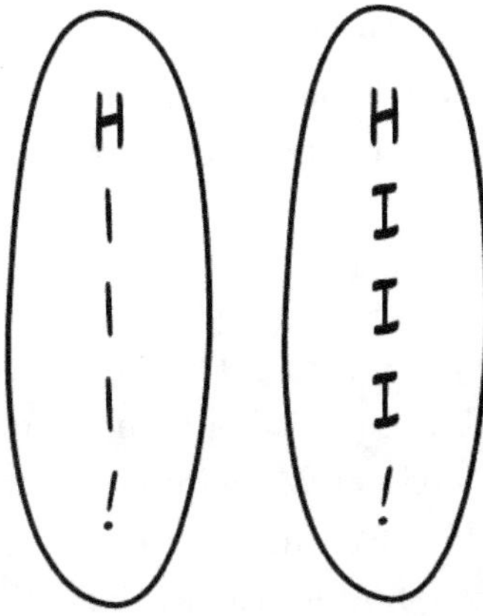

Figure 9: The text "Hiii!" using slashbar I's (left) versus crossbar I's (right). The crossbar I's make the text easier to read and distinguish as the letter I.

In particular, keep an eye on unnecessary commas, commas used in place of hyphens for stutters, brackets used in place of quotation marks, and flipped interrobangs (!? instead of the English-standard ?!). Periods, exclamation marks, and question marks should be used to end sentences even in cases where the Japanese did not have ending punctuation.

Note that some publishers will ask for these peculiarities to be retained. While your editor brain may revolt, check the style guide and review guidelines before you take an editing test to make sure you're not cut from the running over a stylistic preference.

Periods and Abbreviations

While publishers will generally forego the use of periods in abbreviations, periods are used in cases where an abbreviation could be mistaken for a word. For example, *US* (for United States) looks an awful lot like the pronoun *us* in an all-caps dialogue font. In these cases, use periods to avoid confusion.

Dashes

Western comics of the superhero variety traditionally use double dashes (--) rather than an em dash (—), but manga dashes vary by publisher. Many comic fonts are made with the assumption that double dashes are the norm, so the dash character provided may be too short to read as an em dash. If the style guide allows for it, the letterer can be asked to elongate the dash character to make it more closely resemble an em dash.

Ellipses

Three dots or an ellipsis glyph may be used in manga. Usually the publisher style guide and font choice determines which will be used, as some fonts do not have an ellipsis glyph. In either case, do not include spaces between periods in the style of Chicago.

Another important note regarding ellipses is that they are often used to link sentences that span multiple bubbles. Most publishers will use a trailing ellipsis to signal that a sentence continues into another bubble, and some publishers will use additional leading ellipsis at the beginning of the continuation. A few publishers accept

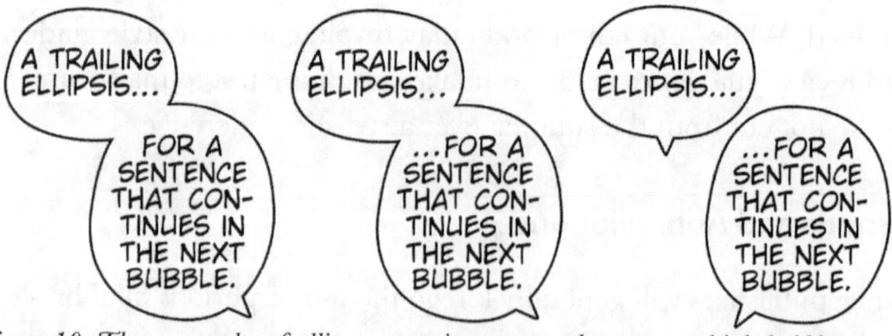

Figure 10: Three examples of ellipses usage in sentences that span multiple bubbles.

commas as ending punctuation in a bubble as well, though the choice is less common and departs from Western comic conventions.

Special Characters and Glyphs

Hearts, stars, squiggles, and other glyphs are often preserved when a manga is published in English, though not all dialogue fonts include these. Some examples of common glyphs are shown in Figure 11.

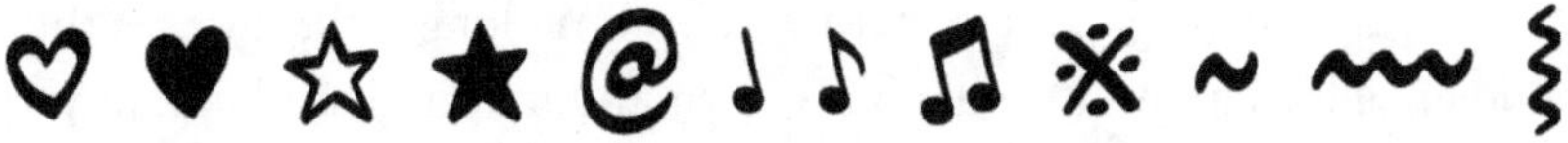

Figure 11: Glyphs from the font Tight Spot BB.

Working in Translation

◇◇◇◇◇

Some decades ago, heavy localization of Japanese media was considered acceptable when bringing works to an English-speaking audience. Character names would sometimes be changed entirely to more American-sounding alternatives and the content of a translation could differ from the source to appeal to an audience without much exposure to Japanese culture. This is no longer the case, as the audience for Japanese media has grown and matured, and in many cases, fans of manga will demand fidelity to the original work. This means that large changes or additions to a manga's narrative or content should be avoided, and developmental editing would not be considered appropriate.

In addition, authors are usually not available to answer questions and cannot be contacted without going through several editors on both the licensee and licensor's sides. So rather than the author, the translator is typically consulted when questions arise in a script. When working with translators, it's important to keep in mind that they usually will not have further insight into characterization and future developments than any other reader. What they can do, however, is read ahead or provide explanations of linguistic clues within the text. The key to working alongside a translator is to phrase queries in such a way that this is acknowledged so the translator will be able to provide a helpful answer. It can also be helpful to have a basic understanding of how Japanese differs from English.

Grammatical Considerations

While English is a subject-verb-object (SVO) language, Japanese is a subject-object-verb (SOV) language, which means most sentences will end with a verb. Because of this, sentences will sometimes need to be flipped, especially when spanning multiple bubbles.

Another consideration to keep in mind is that Japanese is a *null-subject* language, which means that the subject of the sentence can be omitted entirely and still be grammatical. Typically the subject is clear through context, but one of the most common translation errors is assumption of the wrong subject. Usually this will manifest as a logical error in the text, so when in doubt, query.

Most singular and plural nouns are indistinguishable in Japanese, so the number of objects being referred to in a sentence may be unclear. In fact, you've already seen several examples of this in action since *manga* is both a singular and plural noun even in English. When you suspect any confusion, reference the art or check future chapters if there are any available.

Gendered pronouns are less commonly used when speaking about others in Japanese, so the gender of a character can be avoided for multiple pages, chapters, or even volumes of a work. In these cases, it's acceptable to use neutral pronouns such as *they* or *them* when appropriate. Conversely, Japanese has a plethora of first-person I pronouns that can indicate everything from social class to gender. You may see notes from translators about this, and these will need to be omitted entirely, localized, or handled through translation notes on a case-by-case basis.

Stiltedness

Stiltedness can happen when the translator sticks too closely to Japanese turns of phrase and grammar. It becomes a problem when the meaning of the text is indecipherable in English. These issues often come from idioms or in the form of not-quite-grammatical word order that will need to be entirely rephrased.

Some translators, especially newer ones, are more sensitive about staying faithful to the original text and will be less willing to let go of stilted phrases. But Japanese typically doesn't read awkwardly to a native speaker, so the stiltedness isn't true to the author's original intent. If a sentence doesn't make sense to you or doesn't seem like a good English construction, it likely won't make sense to the reader and should be rewritten or queried.

Japanese Literacy: How Much Does an Editor Need to Know?

While not all manga editorial jobs require knowledge of Japanese, some familiarity with the most basic writing systems—hiragana and katakana—can significantly help an editor with their job (and be a resume booster). See Appendix A, which has a character chart that can be used when working with hiragana and katakana.

Characterization

In Japanese, manners of speaking and formality are baked into character dialogue and are often shown through sentence endings, which can be used to distinguish speakers. English has some of these register differences (examples: no, nah, yes, yeah, uh-huh, etc.), but they tend to be less prominent than in Japanese. An experienced translator will know how to handle these, but newer translators may need some help with characterization. For a deeper look into formality and speaking styles, take a look at keigo and yakuwarigo.

Honorifics

Japanese features several honorifics that are attached to the end of names with a hyphen (such as Jan-chan or Jan Cash-san). Some publishers will want to keep these in all cases while others will want them turned into English equivalents. You may also see some nicknames that make use of honorifics without a hyphen. For example, Icchan and Akkun are pronounced with a stressed sound at the *cc* and *kk* syllables and are different from I-chan or A-kun. These will typically be handled by the translator.

Glossaries, Series Bibles, Term Lists, Oh My!

Publishers often keep a list of terms that need to be consistent within the translation of a series (such as character names), similar to how a style guide would have a word list. Usually these list the original Japanese, the phonetic reading (often called the *romaji* or *ruby*), page or chapter where the word was first used, and other relevant notes. In some cases, the category of term (character, object, location, etc.) may also be included. These term lists are usually organized as a spreadsheet rather than as a style sheet.

Often these lists are used not only by the publisher and its freelancers but also by companies making novel, anime, or movie adaptations of the series. As timelines are tight for most types of media, it's important to provide a complete term list to be used by these other entities. Otherwise, if the translators and editors are not consistent between projects, the preexisting terms might be disregarded entirely in favor of creating new terms and spellings.

Translation Notes

Translation notes are additions to the text that were not present in the original Japanese manga but explain elements that may otherwise be lost in translation. Each note will disrupt the reading experience, so most publishers opt for chapter or volume endnotes without asterisks, though some include notes in the gutters between panels for signs and other elements that are essential to the manga's story.

Working with Letterers

◇◇◇◇◇

Letterers usually work from the text script into the Adobe Suite. Most publishers will require letterers to work primarily in InDesign to create a print-ready book, though letterers will also work in Photoshop, Clip Studio Paint (CSP), or other programs as well.

A letterer's primary role is to typeset the dialogue text and create the sound effects. In addition, they often lay out the art files according to the publisher's print requirements and may redraw (also called *retouch*) minor sections of the artwork when necessary.

Letterers are often given merged art files, meaning that the sound effects and asides within the art are not on separate layers. When the English text doesn't cover sections of the art the original Japanese text did, the letterer needs to redraw the art by hand, so changing a sound effect or other text outside of bubbles after retouching has been done may double a letterer's work—and their annoyance at you. Bubbles also come merged into the artwork and usually cannot be redrawn because they're considered part of the art, so keep text space constraints in mind, and when in doubt, edit text down.

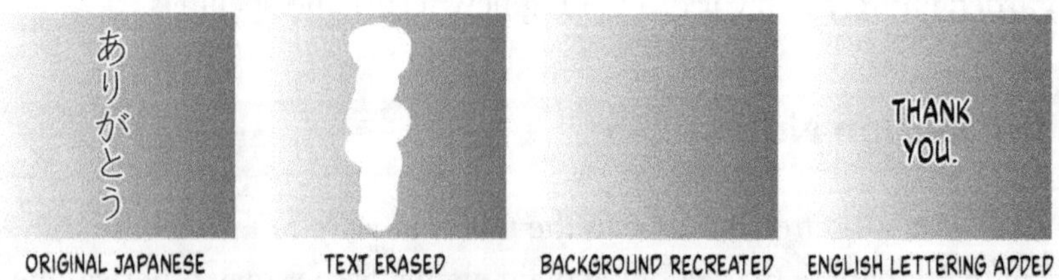

Figure 12: An example of the retouch process. The Japanese text is erased, then the background needs to be recreated anywhere the English text will not cover. In cases where the English text covers a large amount of the background, the whole background might not need to be redrawn.

Sound Effects

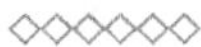

Sound effects (also called *SFX* or *FX*) are the representation of sounds, actions, or emotional states in manga through stylized text. While Western comics focus on physical sounds (wham, bam, pow, etc.), manga have a greater variety of sound effects that can describe anything from a character's mood to the sound of silence.

Japanese sound effects fall into three categories, as shown in Table 1.

Type	Description	Examples
Giseigo	Vocalized onomatopoeia produced by living organisms	ARGH, ROAR, HUFF
Giongo	Sounds produced by inanimate objects	KLATTER, KRASH
Gitaigo	Description of a state of being or motion that is not necessarily a sound	CRICKET CRICKET, SHUFFLE, GLOOM

Table 1: The types of manga sound effects

Each publisher has its own guidelines on how to handle sound effects within the art, but the treatment typically can be placed into one of two categories: *subtitling* and *replacement*.

Subtitling

Subtitled sound effects leave the original Japanese words intact while placing a translation of the effect in close proximity to the Japanese. These can be set in a plain font or stylized to mimic the original effect. It's best practice to angle subtitled sound effects slightly to help unify them with the art and so they appear visually distinct from typeset words and dynamic on the page. While subtitling requires more of the art to be covered and might pose difficulties due to space constraints, it is less time intensive for the letterer than full replacement.

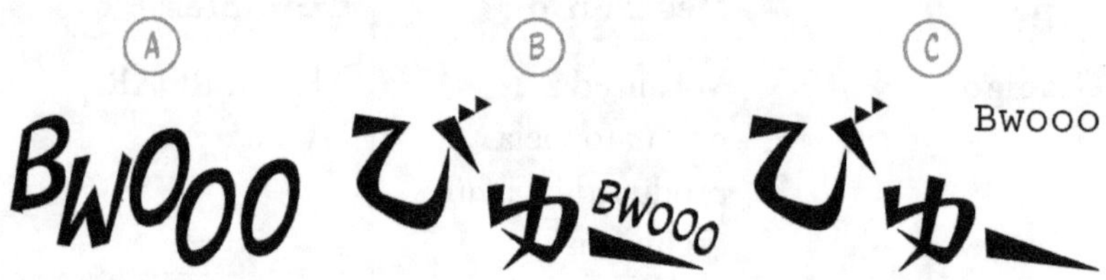

Figure 13: An example of full replacement (A), subtitling (B), and an undesirable way of rendering a sound effect (C). While A and B would be acceptable methods of localizing a sound effect, leaving example C in a book might have readers bwooing the publisher!

Replacement

The original Japanese sound effect is erased and replaced by an English equivalent that is stylized to look similar to the original Japanese. This is labor intensive for the letterer, as the Japanese effects need to be erased and any areas that are not covered by the new English effect must be redrawn or retouched by the letterer.

Editors should be aware of what they are asking when requesting a letterer change an effect, as some letterers may hand-letter the

English effects, which means they are not using easily replaceable fonts and must redo the entire effect when a change is requested.

Rules of Thumb for Editing Sound Effects

When adapting sound effects, try to find options that seem like sounds rather than words. Here are some tips:

- Avoid nouns or adjectives in most cases.
- Use onomatopoeia whenever possible.
- Use verbs when an onomatopoeia doesn't exist.
- Avoid using present-tense verbs.

For example, a translator may render a sound effect in a script as "sits." A better way of handling this would be to use an onomatopoeia such as "tunk," which communicates the same meaning when paired with artwork that already shows a character sitting down.

Asides can be mistaken for sound effects and the distinction between the two can sometimes be blurred. Asides are typically handwritten or in a font that resembles handwriting, and they are usually complete sentences. They may also be in a mixed-case font in English.

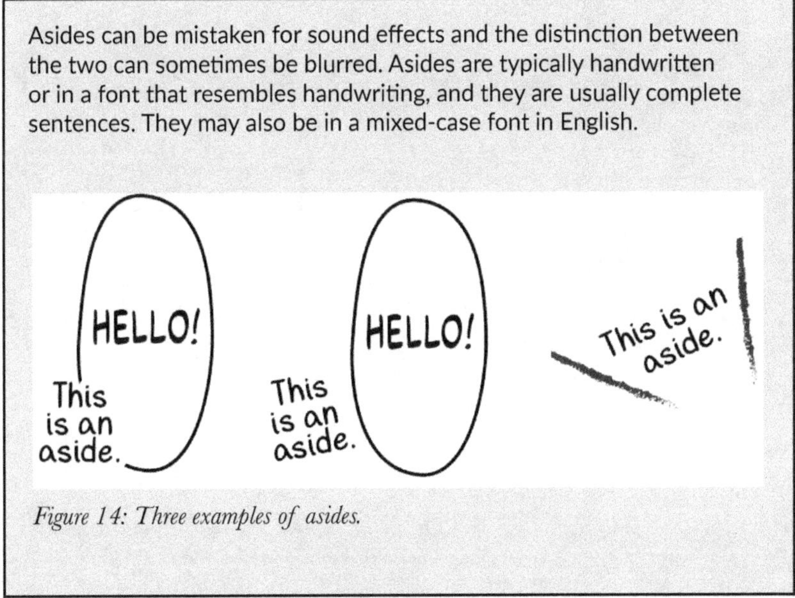

Figure 14: Three examples of asides.

For another example, if "silence" is used as a sound effect for the lack of any sound, it may be better to use "cricket cricket" for a comedic scene or "hush" for a scene that carries more gravity.

Removing the vowels from a word or substituting letters can make a sound effect seem less like a word and more like an onomatopoeia. For example, the letter C can be replaced with the letter K (crash → krash) or the vowels can be removed (rumble → rmmb).

Like dialogue fonts, sound effects generally shouldn't be rendered in serif fonts and fonts used for prose. You usually will not need to worry about font choices, as these are typically handled by the letterer or dictated in a style guide, but technical issues can sometimes result in a font changing unintentionally, which will need to be queried.

Print Layout

◇◇◇◇◇

You are generally less likely to work with InDesign pages as a free-lancer and more likely to work with them as an in-house editor, but it is still helpful to understand the fundamentals of the print layout so you know why you are pointing out types of issues while editing.

When pages are cut at a printer, the cuts are not always exact, so unless a white border around the art is intended, the artwork needs to extend past the trim lines to create what is called a *bleed*. This ensures that the artwork will reach the edge of the pages when it is cut. The area of the page within the margin is guaranteed not to be cut, so it is called the *safe area*. This is where all the text of the manga should go to guarantee it isn't lost in the printer's garbage bin.

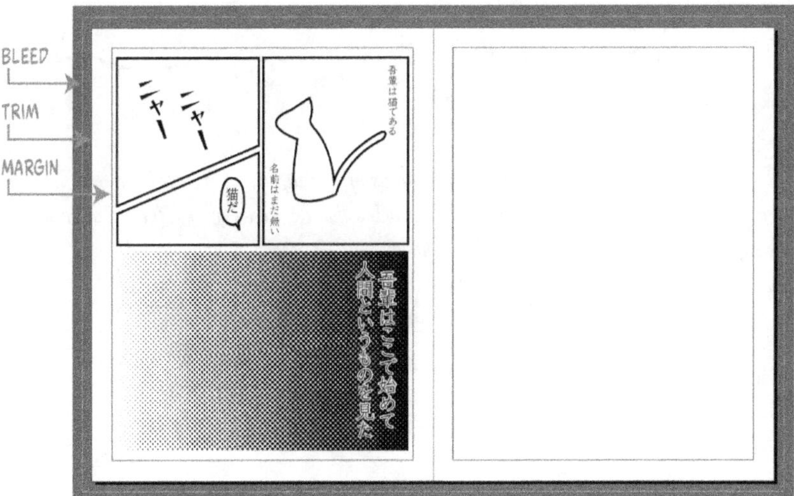

Figure 15: A screenshot of a spread from InDesign.

In some cases, the Japanese artist may publish their work for digital distribution without taking the bleed into account, so the text in bubbles that venture into the edge of a page needs to be moved into the safe area in the English release. Though the text will look unbalanced, this is necessary to avoid cutting off the text when the pages are trimmed for print. If you are working on pages that are for a digital-only publication, you will not need to worry about this.

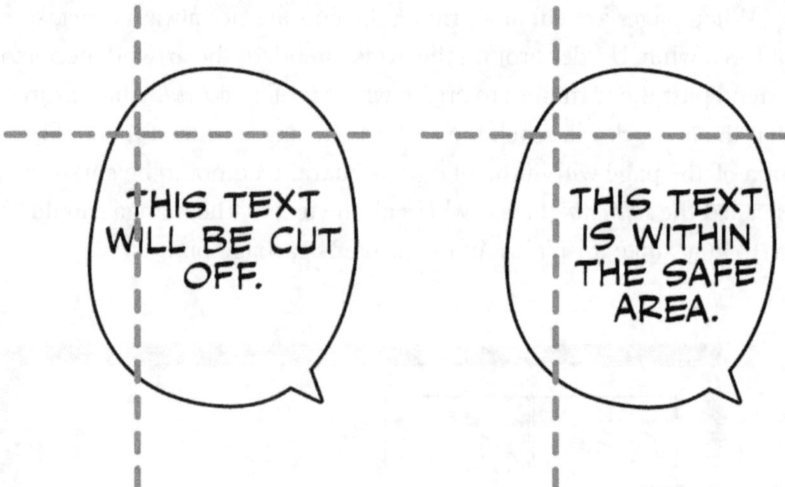

Figure 16: The dotted lines represent the bounds of the safe area. The text beyond the safe area (left) could be trimmed off during printing, so the text needs to be adjusted to be within the safety (right) even though the bubble appears unbalanced.

AI, Machine Translation, and Automated Systems

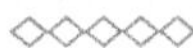

While new manga technology is emerging with the promise of reducing or improving workflows, the software is often created to appeal to companies rather than the individuals using it.

For freelancers, editing machine-translated text will usually result in the same amount of work or more than working with a human translator, so avoid these jobs, especially when the client expects a discounted rate.

For in-house editors and managers reading this guide, many translators and letterers find machine translation (MTL) and specialized manga software to be cumbersome if not disruptive to their established workflows. In addition, AI may use data fed into it to train future output, which may run afoul of licensor agreements. Proceed with caution and due diligence when using these systems.

Proofreading Tips and Tricks

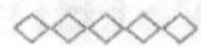

This section goes over some common proofreading issues you may encounter in manga.

Duplicated Text

Bubbles end up with identical text in adjacent bubbles. These should generally be flagged since they are highly likely to be errors.

Why This Happens

Some letterers copy and paste from the script into text boxes, and human error sometimes results in duplications.

Formatting Issues

The bubbles in the lettered version do not have bold or italics formatting that was included in the script.

Why This Happens

A script's formatting will not necessarily be retained when pasted into InDesign. The letterer typically has to manually apply all bold, italics, and other formatting by hand, so these can be missed during the lettering stage.

Text Doesn't Match the Art

The text directly contradicts the art or seems divorced from the reality shown in the art. For example, the dialogue may say, "Put your hands up!" even though the art only shows the character putting one hand up.

Why This Happens

When translating or editing in text-based software, those working directly from a script can miss context clues in the art. Japanese also doesn't require singular and plural nouns to be distinguished from each other, so the number of items being referred to in a sentence can be ambiguous when referencing only the text.

Misattributed Speaker

The flow of conversation seems to make a logical leap or is a non sequitur.

Why This Happens

Depending on how the script was translated and edited, the translator or previous editors may have mistaken the speaker of a line of dialogue. These generally need to be queried so they can be checked against the Japanese.

Breaking Balloon boundaries

The text overlaps the boundaries of its container.

Why This Happens

Dialogue sometimes simply won't fit in a bubble. But breaking the bubble's boundaries is distracting to the reader and one of the gravest sins a manga publisher can commit. In these cases, the text can be edited down, the words can be broken up by syllable with hyphens, or the font size can be bumped down. Your role as proofreader is to corral the words back into their prisons lest they assault the eyes of the reader.

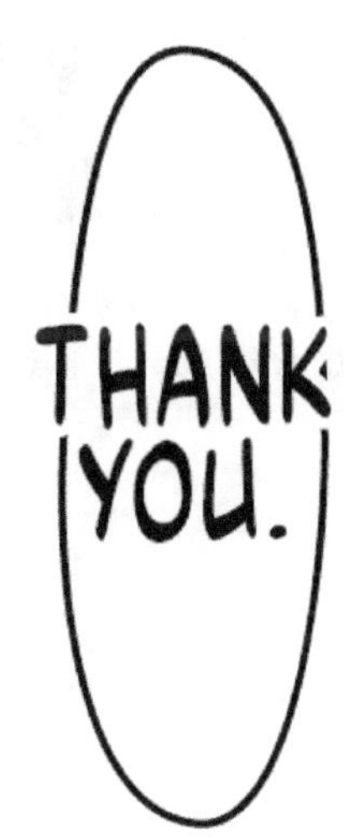

Figure 17: Oversized dialogue text that escapes the boundaries of the bubble's borders.

Kerning Issues

Kerning is the space between letters. In some cases, the default kerning of a font might not be ideal for all character combinations and will make the reader do a double take to see whether they understood the text properly.

Why This Happens

The letters are too close together and have created an abomination. L-I combinations are especially prone to these issues. R-N can also form an M in lowercase or vice versa, rendering an innocent "pom" into a much naughtier word! Keep sound effects in all caps and ask the letterer to adjust the kerning—they'll generally know what to do.

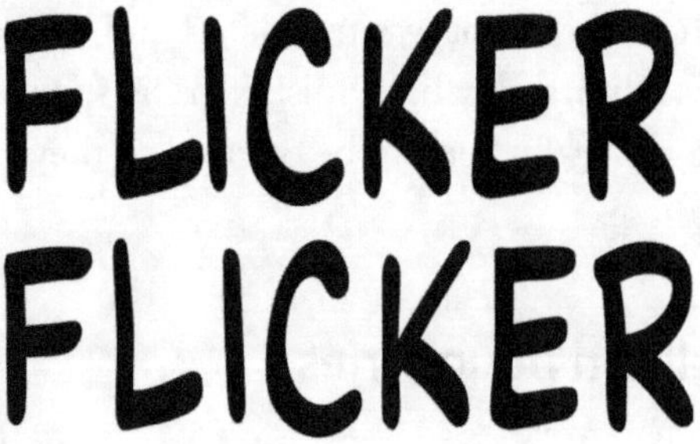

FLICKER
FLICKER

Figure 18: The word flicker *shown using different kerning options. Kerning that is too close can result in letters merging and being read as an unintended word.*

Finding Work

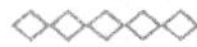

In-house manga jobs sometimes show up in publisher job listings such as Publishers Weekly's JobZone. For those starting out their career, Penguin Random House often has spring internships listed on their careers website and, while the internships are not for specific publishers, noting an interest in manga may lead you to one of the publishers you desire, should you be accepted.

For freelance jobs, the best way to apply is by sending inquiries regardless of whether a job posting is listed. In some cases, publishers receive enough solicitations via email that they do not need to post recruitment ads or position listings. A web page listing publishers that hire for manga can be found in Appendix B. I also run an intermittent newsletter with job postings, which can likewise be found in Appendix B. The previous newsletter posts are available in the archive and can be used to find the websites where publishers commonly post their jobs.

Social media and social events such as talks and conventions are also a great way to network with others in the industry. Many people within the manga industry have accounts on Twitter and Discord as well. You can find a list of potential organizations to join in Appendix B.

The best way to enter the industry is to reach out, whether to publishers or individuals. If you have any additional questions or simply want to say you found this booklet useful, please feel free to email me at me@janmitsuko.cash.

Appendix A: Hiragana, Katakana, and Kanji

◇◇◇◇◇

Instead of an alphabet, Japanese consists of three character sets: kanji, hiragana, and katakana. Japanese features over two thousand commonly used kanji, which are pictograms that were adopted from the Chinese writing system. Because of kanji's complicated history, each character has multiple pronunciations and combinations with other characters that form words. Later, hiragana and katakana, which are both phonetic writing systems, were adopted alongside kanji, so all three writing systems are used in combination in modern Japanese.

Kanji takes years to master, so we won't cover it here, but hiragana and katakana can easily be learned within a few days or weeks—and in even better news, the hiragana and katakana syllabaries are identical, meaning they're simply two ways of writing the same exact set of sounds. We won't cover all the details here, as that would require a second booklet, but I encourage you to see Appendix B for approachable resources that will help you learn both. Even if you choose not to learn either, this booklet has basic information that will help you navigate how to talk to translators as well as a lookup table that can be used to type out characters so you can look up sound effects or simple words.

Furigana and Ruby

Both hiragana and katakana are often used to provide the phonetic reading of kanji for those learning to read. These phonetic readings are placed alongside the kanji as *ruby* (or *rubi*) annotations and are called *furigana*. Romaji, mentioned earlier in the booklet, is the phonetic reading in Latin script.

In some cases, instead of providing the furigana reading for kanji, authors will make use of ruby to give a word a secondary meaning—the translator will usually note when this is the case or will include a note in the term sheet or glossary.

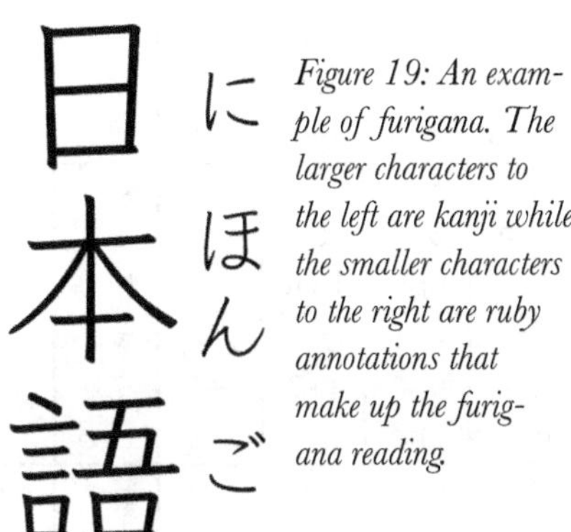

Figure 19: An example of furigana. The larger characters to the left are kanji while the smaller characters to the right are ruby annotations that make up the furigana reading.

Hiragana and Katakana Lookup Tables

Hiragana is used for most Japanese words, so compared with katakana, you are more likely to see this character set in furigana and nested among kanji. Meanwhile, katakana is mostly used to write loan words into Japanese. The characters have a slightly sharper look to them compared with hiragana, so the characters are

ん/ン n	わ/ワ wa	ら/ラ ra	や/ヤ ya	ま/マ ma	は/ハ ha	な/ナ na	た/タ ta	さ/サ sa	か/カ ka	あ/ア a
		り/リ ri		み/ミ mi	ひ/ヒ hi	に/ニ ni	ち/チ chi	し/シ shi	き/キ ki	い/イ i
		る/ル ru	ゆ/ユ yu	む/ム mu	ふ/フ fu	ぬ/ヌ nu	つ/ツ tsu	す/ス su	く/ク ku	う/ウ u
		れ/レ re		め/メ me	へ/ヘ he	ね/ネ ne	て/テ te	せ/セ se	け/ケ ke	え/エ e
	を/ヲ wo	ろ/ロ ro	よ/ヨ yo	も/モ mo	ほ/ホ ho	の/ノ no	と/ト to	そ/ソ so	こ/コ ko	お/オ o

Table 2: Hiragana, katakana, and the keyboard character combinations needed to type them out. The left character is the hiragana version and the right character after the slash is katakana.

みゃ/ ミャ mya	ちゃ/ チャ cha	ひゃ/ ヒャ hya	しゃ/ シャ sha	きゃ/ キャ kya	ぱ/パ pa	ば/バ ba	だ/ダ da	ざ/ザ za	が/ガ ga	あ/ア xa
みゅ/ ミュ myu	ちゅ/ チュ chu	ひゅ/ ヒュ hyu	しゅ/ シュ shu	きゅ/ キュ kyu	ぴ/ピ pi	び/ビ bi	ぢ/ヂ ji	じ/ジ ji	ぎ/ギ gi	い/イ xi
みょ/ ミョ myo	ちょ/ チョ cho	ひょ/ ヒョ hyo	しょ/ ショ sho	きょ/ キョ kyo	ぷ/プ pu	ぶ/ブ bu	づ/ヅ du	ず/ズ zu	ぐ/グ gu	う/ウ xu
にゃ/ ニャ nya	りゃ/ リャ rya	びゃ/ ビャ bya	じゃ/ ジャ jya	ぎゃ/ ギャ gya	ぺ/ペ pe	べ/ベ be	で/デ de	ぜ/ゼ ze	げ/ゲ ge	え/エ xe
にゅ/ ニュ nyu	りゅ/ リュ ryu	びゅ/ ビュ byu	じゅ/ ジュ jyu	ぎゅ/ ギュ gyu	ぽ/ポ po	ぼ/ボ bo	ど/ド do	ぞ/ゾ zo	ご/ゴ go	お/オ xo
にょ/ ニョ nyo	りょ/ リョ ryo	びょ/ ビョ byo	じょ/ ジョ jyo	ぎょ/ ギョ gyo						

Table 3: Additional hiragana and katakana sound combinations that can be formed by combining characters and diacritic marks called dakuten *and* handakuten.

also used to achieve an eerie or discordant effect with "robotic" or "spooky" dialogue.

Japanese has only five vowel sounds represented in its syllabaries, which are the long versions of a, e, i, o, and u. Most sounds are pronounced as they're written in Table 2 and Table 3, except for the mini-vowel set (rightmost column of Table 3), which are typed out with a preceding "x" in order to distinguish them from the full-width vowel set. With this table and an *input method editor* (IME), you will be able to look up characters and type them out, which will also enable you to look up sound effects and simple words online or in dictionaries.

Enabling IME for Text Input

In order to type in Japanese, you'll need to enable your input method editor. You do not need to install any special software to do this, as computers come with the ability to type in multiple languages by default.

Windows instructions

1. Go to **Start** button > **Settings** > **Time & Language** > **Language**
2. Click the **+** sign next to **Add a language**
3. Search for **Japanese** and once the option is selected, click **Next**, then click **Install**

Mac instructions

1. Go to **Settings** > **Keyboard**
2. Click the **+** sign
3. Select **Japanese** from the list and select only **Japanese – Romaji**, then click **Add**

If everything went as expected, your toolbar should show your current keyboard language, and you will now be able to toggle between English and Japanese to type. Some Macs have a language key that looks like a globe, which will also toggle between the keyboard languages.

After selecting the Japanese input mode from the list in the toolbar shown in Figure 20, type the English key combinations from Table 2 or Table 3. A drop-down list should appear with the

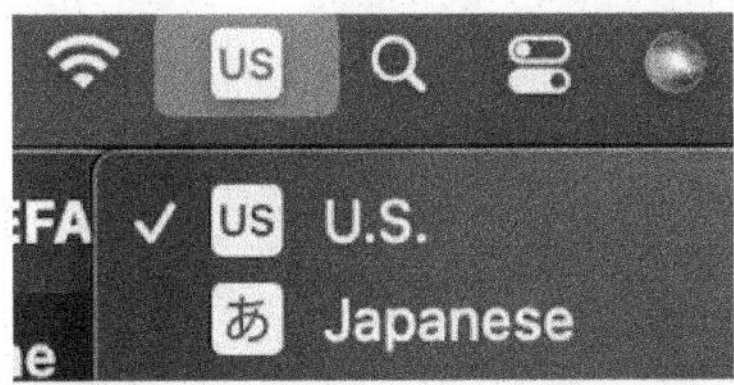

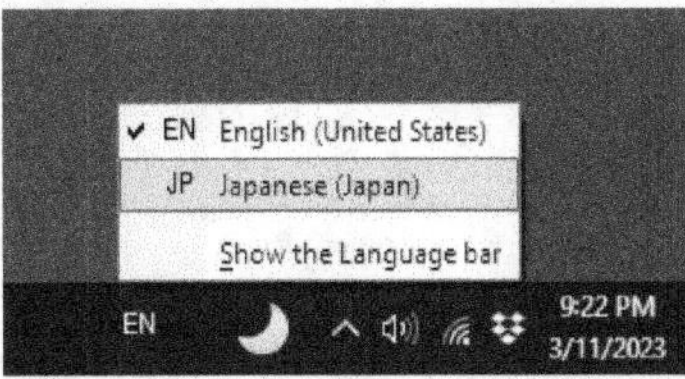

Figure 20: The IME selection lists in Mac and Windows that will show up on the toolbar

characters, which you can select using arrow keys or by pressing your spacebar. Pressing enter will select the character so you can type another.

Appendix B: Other Resources

Hiragana and Katakana

Learn Hiragana
Link: tofugu.com/japanese/learn-hiragana
A primer on hiragana.

Learn Katakana
Link: tofugu.com/japanese/learn-katakana
A similar primer on katakana.

Dictionaries

Jisho.org
Link: jisho.org
Likely the most widely used free Japanese-to-English dictionary.

Yakuaru
Link: yakuaru.com
An open glossary of terms and translations used in media.

Jaded Network
Link: thejadednetwork.com/sfx
The most widely used Japanese sound effect database. The website is old, but the search function still works.

Comic Book FX
Link: comicbookfx.com/index.php
Examples of sound effects from Western comic books.

Jan's Sound Effect Database

Link: janmitsuko.cash/resources/translation-resources/japanese-sfx-database
My continually updated database of sound effects.

Lettering References

Blambot's website

Link: blambot.com/pages/lettering-tips
Lettering guidelines by American comic letterer Nate Piekos. Some of these tips will not be applicable to manga, but many manga letterers use Blambot's fonts and guides.

Sara Linsley's Lettering Guides

Link: github.com/saraoswald/lettering-tutorials/wiki
Lettering guides written by former manga letterer Sara Linsley for other manga letterers.

Manga Lettering: Translating What Can't Be Spoken Workshop by Sara Linsley

Link: sara.pizza/presentations/Manga%20Lettering%20-%20Translating%20What%20Cant%20Be%20Spoken.pdf

Manga Fonts

Link: mangafonts.carrd.co
Real examples of fonts used in manga.

Manga Lettering and Translation

Link: swet.jp/members/article/manga_lettering_and_translation
An article with a discussion between three manga letterers about their processes.

Comic and Manga Fonts

Comicraft
Link: comicbookfonts.com

Blambot
Link: blambot.com

Sara Linsley's Fonts
Link: ko-fi.com/salinsley/shop

Aidan Clarke's Font
Link: ko-fi.com/aidanclarke/shop

Other Tools and References

KanjiTomo
Link: kanjitomo.net
An OCR tool that can identify Japanese characters in images, which can be helpful for copying and pasting words to look them up in a dictionary. This tool does not work for handwritten text.

Related Words.io
Link: relatedwords.io
A tool that finds words with associated meanings. Useful for word-play, which frequently shows up in manga.

Power Thesaurus
Link: powerthesaurus.org
A thesaurus created through user submissions. Useful for finding a word when the dictionary definition of a translation isn't quite right.

Merriam-Webster Thesaurus

Link: merriam-webster.com/thesaurus
Merriam-Webster's free online thesaurus. Words can be searched for based on their parts of speech.

Japanese Name Enders: More than Mr. and Ms.

Link: tofugu.com/japanese/name-enders
A primer on Japanese honorifics.

Job Listings and Publisher Lists

Jan's List of Publishers

Link: janmitsuko.cash/resources/list-of-publishers
A list of publishers that license manga in English.

Publishers Weekly JobZone

Link: jobzone.publishersweekly.com
A general listing for publishing jobs. Many in-house manga jobs are posted here.

Jan's Email Newsletter

Link: janmitsuko.cash/newsletter
Includes a list of recent job listings in each post

Groups and Social Media

Comic Book Editors Alliance

Link: facebook.com/groups/comicbookeditorsalliance
A Facebook group of comic book editors.

HonYaks

Link: hon-yaks.com

A localization group dedicated to experienced and aspiring professionals. Though the group is focused on video game translation, many manga professionals have also joined.

SWET – Society of Writers, Editors, and Translators

Link: swet.jp

A membership group of professionals focused on Japanese translation.

Further Reading and Watching

Leaving "Dattebayo" Untranslated: NARUTO Editor and Translator Share the Complex Challenges Involved in the Manga's Localization

Link: naruto-official.com/en/news/01_1401?nolangsuggestion=1

So You Want to be a Manga Editor? | WonderCon@Home 2021

Link: youtube.com/watch?v=dcHfzu6Whb8

Meet the Manga Editors: The Philosophy and Practice of Manga Editing

Link: youtube.com/watch?v=cvBOg1Jer_E

EFA's Comics and Graphic Novel Conventions for Proofreaders Webinar

Link: the-efa.org/product/comics-and-graphic-novel-conventions-for-proofreaders-webinar-recording

Acknowledgments

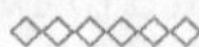

Thank you to all the translators, editors, and letterers who have made free resources available online, especially Sara Linsley, whose tutorials are as lovely as she is. Thank you also to David Evelyn and Brandon Bovia for putting up with the many unsolicited example images I sent and for your feedback.

Author Bio

◇◇◇◇◇

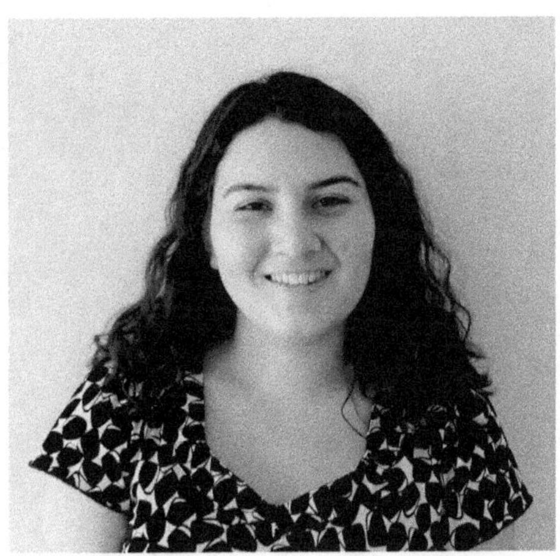

Jan Mitsuko Cash is a freelance editor and translator of Japanese fiction with much too much to do and much too little time on her hands. She has helped bring over a hundred volumes of Japanese novels and manga into English and has assisted others with starting their careers in the localization industry.